THE CHATSWOR
GARDEN DIARY 2007

THE DOWAGER DUCHESS OF DEVONSHIRE

PHOTOGRAPHS BY GARY ROGERS

F

FRANCES LINCOLN LIMITED
PUBLISHERS

Frances Lincoln Limited
4 Torriano Mews
Torriano Avenue
London NW5 2RZ
www.franceslincoln.com

The Chatsworth Garden Diary 2007
Copyright © Frances Lincoln Limited 2006
Text © Deborah Devonshire
Photographs © Gary Rogers

Astronomical information reproduced, with permission, from data
supplied by HM Nautical Almanac Office, copyright © Council for
the Central Laboratory of the Research Councils.

British Library cataloguing-in-publication data
A catalogue record for this book is available from
the British Library

ISBN 10: 0-7112-2625-3
ISBN 13: 978-0-7112-2625-8

Printed in China

First Frances Lincoln edition 2006

Cover
Front: The West Front, showing the gilded windows, and the West
Garden in the late afternoon
Back: Water sprays up through two small jets in the pool in front of
the Cascade House before tumbling down the steps of the Cascade.

Title page: *Berberis wilsoniae* in the Rock Garden

Right: The Cascade from Thomas Archer's Cascade House of 1711

VISITORS' INFORMATION

Chatsworth is open daily from mid
March to December. Please visit
the website www.chatsworth.org
or telephone 01246 565300 for
further information, opening times
and prices.

CALENDAR 2007

JANUARY	FEBRUARY	MARCH	APRIL	MAY	JUNE
M T W T F S S	M T W T F S S	M T W T F S S	M T W T F S S	M T W T F S S	M T W T F S S
1 2 3 4 5 6 7	1 2 3 4	1 2 3 4	1	1 2 3 4 5 6	1 2 3
8 9 10 11 12 13 14	5 6 7 8 9 10 11	5 6 7 8 9 10 11	2 3 4 5 6 7 8	7 8 9 10 11 12 13	4 5 6 7 8 9 10
15 16 17 18 19 20 21	12 13 14 15 16 17 18	12 13 14 15 16 17 18	9 10 11 12 13 14 15	14 15 16 17 18 19 20	11 12 13 14 15 16 17
22 23 24 25 26 27 28	19 20 21 22 23 24 25	19 20 21 22 23 24 25	16 17 18 19 20 21 22	21 22 23 24 25 26 27	18 19 20 21 22 23 24
29 30 31	26 27 28	26 27 28 29 30 31	23 24 25 26 27 28 29	28 29 30 31	25 26 27 28 29 30
			30		

JULY	AUGUST	SEPTEMBER	OCTOBER	NOVEMBER	DECEMBER
M T W T F S S	M T W T F S S	M T W T F S S	M T W T F S S	M T W T F S S	M T W T F S S
1	1 2 3 4 5	1 2	1 2 3 4 5 6 7	1 2 3 4	1 2
2 3 4 5 6 7 8	6 7 8 9 10 11 12	3 4 5 6 7 8 9	8 9 10 11 12 13 14	5 6 7 8 9 10 11	3 4 5 6 7 8 9
9 10 11 12 13 14 15	13 14 15 16 17 18 19	10 11 12 13 14 15 16	15 16 17 18 19 20 21	12 13 14 15 16 17 18	10 11 12 13 14 15 16
16 17 18 19 20 21 22	20 21 22 23 24 25 26	17 18 19 20 21 22 23	22 23 24 25 26 27 28	19 20 21 22 23 24 25	17 18 19 20 21 22 23
23 24 25 26 27 28 29	27 28 29 30 31	24 25 26 27 28 29 30	29 30 31	26 27 28 29 30	24 25 26 27 28 29 30
30 31					31

CALENDAR 2008

JANUARY	FEBRUARY	MARCH	APRIL	MAY	JUNE
M T W T F S S	M T W T F S S	M T W T F S S	M T W T F S S	M T W T F S S	M T W T F S S
1 2 3 4 5 6	1 2 3	1 2	1 2 3 4 5 6	1 2 3 4	1
7 8 9 10 11 12 13	4 5 6 7 8 9 10	3 4 5 6 7 8 9	7 8 9 10 11 12 13	5 6 7 8 9 10 11	2 3 4 5 6 7 8
14 15 16 17 18 19 20	11 12 13 14 15 16 17	10 11 12 13 14 15 16	14 15 16 17 18 19 20	12 13 14 15 16 17 18	9 10 11 12 13 14 15
21 22 23 24 25 26 27	18 19 20 21 22 23 24	17 18 19 20 21 22 23	21 22 23 24 25 26 27	19 20 21 22 23 24 25	16 17 18 19 20 21 22
28 29 30 31	25 26 27 28 29	24 25 26 27 28 29 30	28 29 30	26 27 28 29 30 31	23 24 25 26 27 28 29
		31			30

JULY	AUGUST	SEPTEMBER	OCTOBER	NOVEMBER	DECEMBER
M T W T F S S	M T W T F S S	M T W T F S S	M T W T F S S	M T W T F S S	M T W T F S S
1 2 3 4 5 6	1 2 3	1 2 3 4 5 6 7	1 2 3 4 5	1 2	1 2 3 4 5 6 7
7 8 9 10 11 12 13	4 5 6 7 8 9 10	8 9 10 11 12 13 14	6 7 8 9 10 11 12	3 4 5 6 7 8 9	8 9 10 11 12 13 14
14 15 16 17 18 19 20	11 12 13 14 15 16 17	15 16 17 18 19 20 21	13 14 15 16 17 18 19	10 11 12 13 14 15 16	15 16 17 18 19 20 21
21 22 23 24 25 26 27	18 19 20 21 22 23 24	22 23 24 25 26 27 28	20 21 22 23 24 25 26	17 18 19 20 21 22 23	22 23 24 25 26 27 28
28 29 30 31	25 26 27 28 29 30 31	29 30	27 28 29 30 31	24 25 26 27 28 29 30	29 30 31

INTRODUCTION

Everything at Chatsworth is on a vast scale: house, stables, garden, park, even the landscape in which it stands. Since the time of Queen Elizabeth I, when Bess of Hardwick bought the land, all the aspects controlled by man have evolved to make it what you see today. In its present shape the 105-acre garden is a mongrel product, which has somehow happily settled into a world of its own, accepting the changes that have taken place. A garden by its very nature cannot stay still and Chatsworth has led the fashions of garden design over the years.

Signs of the work of the famous outdoor men – London & Wise, Lancelot 'Capability' Brown and Joseph Paxton – in the seventeenth, eighteenth and nineteenth centuries are easily recognised, as are the additions we made in the twentieth century. The professionals worked closely with their patrons, succeeding dukes of Devonshire, reflecting their wish to beautify the surroundings of the house they loved.

Buildings, statuary, rocks and water are as important on this scale as the trees and flowers. The garden starts with the advantage of being on a slope and the varying heights have been used wisely to allow long views to the north, south and west. It is sheltered from the east by a rocky escarpment covered in trees.

Chatsworth has always been open for people to see. In the 1840s, when the railway reached Rowsley, 80,000 came to wonder at Paxton's new glasshouse (the prototype for the Crystal Palace and the newly installed Emperor Fountain, still the highest gravity fed fountain in the world and capable of throwing a jet nearly 30 feet towards the sky. It became the place for a day out from the neighbouring big towns, starting a tradition which many families keep alive today.

There is great variety – huge lawns where children and dogs can run and enjoy themselves, a maze, streams, waterfalls and fountains and changing views over Capability Brown's park to the distant hills of the High Peak. The greenhouses are famed for camellias in spring and grapes in the autumn, and the kitchen garden covering nearly 3 acres (constructed in 1994) is unique with its raised beds and radial planting. A sensory garden was created in 2003 at the suggestion of my grandson William Burlington, and is of interest all the year.

Gary's photographs give a taste of what is to be found in different seasons. He has spent many days here with his camera and this diary is a tribute to his skill.

My son and daughter-in-law have now taken over and it is their turn to leave their mark on the garden.

Deborah Devon
17 March

A midsummer view over the park, from the

JANUARY

WEEK 1

1 MONDAY

4 THURSDAY

---

2 TUESDAY

Holiday, Scotland and New Zealand

5 FRIDAY

---

3 WEDNESDAY

FULL MOON

6 SATURDAY

Epiphany

---

7 SUNDAY

Inside the Display Greenhouse. The spare table top of Sheldon marble – which is quarried five miles from Chatsworth – supports daturas in pots which come into the house when flowering. A tree fern (*Dicksonia antarctica*), lemons and *Brunfelsia pauciflora* grow in this Mediterranean climate.

JANUARY

WEEK 2

8 MONDAY	**12** FRIDAY
9 TUESDAY	**13** SATURDAY
10 WEDNESDAY	**14** SUNDAY
11 THURSDAY LAST QUARTER	

Flora and Aesculapius, nineteenth-century marble copies from the Antique, at the entrance on the North Front drive. The avenue is of tulip trees.

JANUARY

WEEK 3

---

15 MONDAY   Holiday, USA (Martin Luther King's birthday)

18 THURSDAY

16 TUESDAY

19 FRIDAY   NEW MOON

17 WEDNESDAY

20 SATURDAY   Islamic New Year (subject to sighting of the moon)

21 SUNDAY

The West Garden under frost. The reconstruction of the West Garden was begun in 1826, and its architectural bones remain unaltered today.

JANUARY

WEEK 4

22 MONDAY

26 FRIDAY

23 TUESDAY

27 SATURDAY

24 WEDNESDAY

28 SUNDAY

25 THURSDAY   FIRST QUARTER

The bank down to the stream in the Ravine is thick with snowdrops. Hoping to make a blue patch for early spring, we planted squills (*Scilla bifolia*) and glory of the snow (*Chionodoxa*) but nearly all were eaten by pheasants, squirrels and mice, so we have conceded defeat and enjoy the snowdrops, which for some gastronomic reason are spared by these creatures.

29 MONDAY

1 THURSDAY

30 TUESDAY

2 FRIDAY   FULL MOON

31 WEDNESDAY

3 SATURDAY

4 SUNDAY

Germanicus, a nineteenth-century marble statue after the Antique, on the Broad Walk in front of the Conservative Wall. The cupola and its clock surmount James Paine's stable block.

FEBRUARY

WEEK 6

5 MONDAY

9 FRIDAY

6 TUESDAY   Holiday, New Zealand (Waitangi Day)

10 SATURDAY   LAST QUARTER

7 WEDNESDAY

11 SUNDAY

8 THURSDAY

The Sea Horse Fountain on the South Lawn. Triton and the four stone horses were carved by Caius Gabriel Cibber (1630–1700).

FEBRUARY

WEEK 7

---

12 MONDAY   Holiday, USA (Lincoln's birthday) | **15** THURSDAY

13 TUESDAY | **16** FRIDAY

14 WEDNESDAY   St Valentine's Day | **17** SATURDAY   NEW MOON

| **18** SUNDAY   Chinese New Year

Looking through the forsythia pillars in the Rose Garden to the
Salisbury Lawn in early spring

FEBRUARY

WEEK 8

19 MONDAY Holiday, USA (Presidents' Day)	**23** FRIDAY
20 TUESDAY Shrove Tuesday	**24** SATURDAY FIRST QUARTER
21 WEDNESDAY Ash Wednesday	**25** SUNDAY
22 THURSDAY	

The Lion Steps lead down to the South Front from the Broad Walk. They are named after copies of the Medici lions placed here by the 6th Duke of Devonshire in the 1820s.

FEBRUARY MARCH

WEEK 9

26 MONDAY

1 THURSDAY   St David's Day

27 TUESDAY

2 FRIDAY

28 WEDNESDAY

3 SATURDAY   FULL MOON

4 SUNDAY

Daffodils under the weeping ash at the North Front of the house. Many thousands of daffodils have been planted in the grass in different parts of the garden over the years.

MARCH

---

5 MONDAY

9 FRIDAY

---

6 TUESDAY

10 SATURDAY

---

7 WEDNESDAY

11 SUNDAY

---

8 THURSDAY

Looking down at the Cascade House. The 1990s restoration of the Cascade took 10,000 man hours to complete. As much original stone as possible was used.

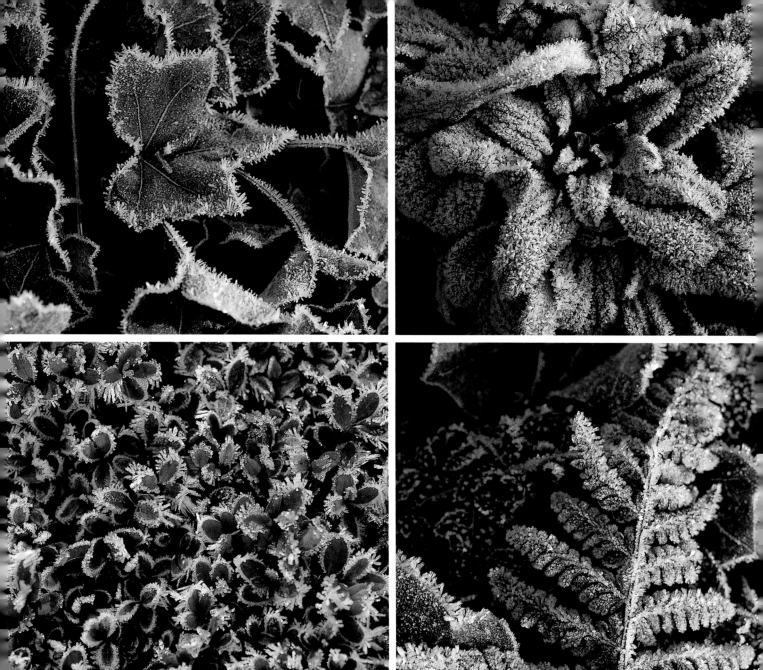

MARCH

WEEK 11

12 MONDAY   Commonwealth Day
LAST QUARTER

15 THURSDAY

13 TUESDAY

16 FRIDAY

14 WEDNESDAY

17 SATURDAY

18 SUNDAY   Mothering Sunday, UK

Clockwise from top left: ivy (*Hedera helix*); lamb's ears (*Stachys lanata*);
fern (*Dryopteris filix-mas*); dwarf box (*Buxus sempervirens* 'Suffruticosa')

MARCH

WEEK 12

19 MONDAY

St Patrick's Day
Holiday, Northern Ireland and Republic of Ireland
NEW MOON

20 TUESDAY

21 WEDNESDAY

Vernal Equinox

22 THURSDAY

23 FRIDAY

24 SATURDAY

25 SUNDAY

British Summertime begins
FIRST QUARTER

The ornamenatal brassicas 'Northern Lights White' and 'Northern Lights Rose' in the Kitchen Garden frames

26 MONDAY

29 THURSDAY

27 TUESDAY

30 FRIDAY

28 WEDNESDAY

31 SATURDAY

1 SUNDAY   Palm Sunday

The pleached limes on the South Lawn that we planted in 1952 to replace rose beds. The statue of the Apollo Belvedere, a nineteenth-century copy after the Antique, faces the Sea Horse Fountain.

APRIL

WEEK 14

2 MONDAY   FULL MOON

3 TUESDAY   Passover (Pesach), First Day

4 WEDNESDAY

5 THURSDAY   Maundy Thursday

6 FRIDAY

Good Friday
Holiday, UK, Republic of Ireland, Canada,
USA, Australia and New Zealand

7 SATURDAY

8 SUNDAY   Easter Sunday

Azaleas by the Grotto Pond; they were planted by Grannie Evie,
my grandmother-in-law, in the 1930s.

APRIL

WEEK 15

9 MONDAY

Easter Monday
Holiday, UK (exc. Scotland), Republic of Ireland,
Canada, Australia and New Zealand
Passover (Pesach), Seventh Day

12 THURSDAY

10 TUESDAY

Passover (Pesach), Eighth Day
LAST QUARTER

13 FRIDAY

11 WEDNESDAY

14 SATURDAY

15 SUNDAY

The Conservative Wall, so called because it conserves heat. It is one of only two glasshouses built by Paxton that remain; the other is the Vinery, near the Potting Shed.

APRIL

WEEK 16

16 MONDAY

20 FRIDAY

17 TUESDAY   NEW MOON

21 SATURDAY   Birthday of Queen Elizabeth II

18 WEDNESDAY

22 SUNDAY

19 THURSDAY

Wisteria floribunda cascading over the ferns and the stone seat on the West Drive

APRIL

WEEK 17

23 MONDAY   St George's Day

24 TUESDAY   FIRST QUARTER

25 WEDNESDAY   Holiday, Australia and New Zealand (Anzac Day)

26 THURSDAY

27 FRIDAY

28 SATURDAY

29 SUNDAY

Camassia flowering near the Trough Waterfall

APRIL ❧ MAY

30 MONDAY

1 TUESDAY

2 WEDNESDAY   FULL MOON

3 THURSDAY

4 FRIDAY

5 SATURDAY

6 SUNDAY

Looking west over the River Derwent and Paine's Bridge to the park. The view was planned and planted by Lancelot 'Capability' Brown in the 1760s; the five oaks in the middle distance ought to be removed as they interfere with Brown's original opening to the horizon.

MAY

7 MONDAY Early May Bank Holiday, UK and Republic of Ireland	**10** THURSDAY LAST QUARTER
8 TUESDAY	**11** FRIDAY
9 WEDNESDAY	**12** SATURDAY
	13 SUNDAY Mother's Day, Canada, USA, Australia and New Zealand

The half-clipped lime hedge which frames the house from the south. The gilt lettering shows the family motto, 'Cavendo Tutus', (Safety through Caution).

MAY

14 MONDAY	**18** FRIDAY
15 TUESDAY	**19** SATURDAY
16 WEDNESDAY NEW MOON	**20** SUNDAY
17 THURSDAY Ascension Day	

Parrot tulips and forget-me-nots in spring, filling the box enclosures of the front garden of the Cottage Garden

MAY

---

21 MONDAY

24 THURSDAY

---

22 TUESDAY

25 FRIDAY

---

23 WEDNESDAY   Jewish Feast of Weeks (Shavuot)
                                              FIRST QUARTER

26 SATURDAY

---

27 SUNDAY   Whit Sunday (Pentecost)

One of two statues of pugilists, copies after Antonio Canova (1757–1822), with a view to the west across the park to New Piece Wood

MAY ❦ JUNE

WEEK 22

28 MONDAY
Spring Bank Holiday, UK
Holiday, USA (Memorial Day)

1 FRIDAY
FULL MOON

29 TUESDAY

2 SATURDAY

30 WEDNESDAY

3 SUNDAY
Trinity Sunday

31 THURSDAY

Russell lupins and Rambler roses in the Conservatory Garden in May

JUNE

WEEK 23

4 MONDAY   Holiday, Republic of Ireland
                               Holiday, New Zealand (The Queen's birthday)

7 THURSDAY   Corpus Christi

5 TUESDAY

8 FRIDAY   LAST QUARTER

6 WEDNESDAY

9 SATURDAY   The Queen's official birthday (subject to confirmation)

10 SUNDAY

The Rose Garden made by my mother-in-law in 1939 in front of the lst Duke's greenhouse. In the nineteenth century this plot was known as the French Garden. The 6th Duke removed the pillars and the seventeeth-century stone busts and urns from the inner court in the house and placed them here.

JUNE

WEEK 24

11 MONDAY · Holiday, Australia (The Queen's birthday)

12 TUESDAY

13 WEDNESDAY

14 THURSDAY

15 FRIDAY · NEW MOON

16 SATURDAY

17 SUNDAY · Father's Day, UK, Canada and USA

Hercules swings his club, in the direction of the Borghese Gladiator (see Week 28). The plants in the border include *Rosa* 'Albertine', *Delphinium* Black Knight Group and *D.* 'Blue Jay', *Geranium psilostemon* and *G.* 'Ann Folkard', *Sisyrinchium striatum*, *Thalictrum flavum* subsp. *glaucum*, Russell lupins and 'Mrs Sinkins' pinks.

JUNE

WEEK 25

18 MONDAY

21 THURSDAY   Summer Solstice

19 TUESDAY

22 FRIDAY   FIRST QUARTER

20 WEDNESDAY

23 SATURDAY

24 SUNDAY

Honeysuckle on the wall overlooking the nineteenth-century raised beds in the West Garden

JUNE ❧ JULY

25 MONDAY

29 FRIDAY

26 TUESDAY

30 SATURDAY   FULL MOON

27 WEDNESDAY

1 SUNDAY

28 THURSDAY

Two of the eight 'stone baskets' in the West Garden built by Wyatville for the 6th Duke in the 1820s. The original golden yew 'cushions' fill the corners, and we have added the sharply clipped box and a central dark green yew. Roses clamber over the balustrade in the foreground.

JULY

2 MONDAY — Holiday, Canada (Canada Day)

3 TUESDAY

4 WEDNESDAY — Holiday, USA (Independence Day)

The orange borders early in the season, backed by large-leaved red oaks (*Quercus rubra*)

5 THURSDAY — MOON

6 FRIDAY

7 SATURDAY — LAST QUARTER

8 SUNDAY

JULY

WEEK 28

9 MONDAY

13 FRIDAY

10 TUESDAY

14 SATURDAY   NEW MOON

11 WEDNESDAY

15 SUNDAY   St Swithin's Day

12 THURSDAY   Holiday, Northern Ireland (Battle of the Boyne)

Thalictrum flavum subsp. *glaucum*, *Geranium psilostemon* and *Rosa* 'Albertine' in the border against the bastion wall in the West Garden

JULY

WEEK 29

16 MONDAY

17 TUESDAY

18 WEDNESDAY

19 THURSDAY

20 FRIDAY

21 SATURDAY

22 SUNDAY   FIRST QUARTER

Sweet peas, grown for cutting, climbing over a wigwam in the
Kitchen Garden, with distant views of the park and woods

JULY

WEEK 30

23 MONDAY

24 TUESDAY

25 WEDNESDAY

26 THURSDAY

27 FRIDAY

28 SATURDAY

29 SUNDAY

The Broad Walk that runs along the East Front of the house is bordered on one side by a hedge of 'Hidcote' lavender enclosing Iceberg roses and clipped golden yew.

JULY ❧ AUGUST

WEEK 31

30 MONDAY FULL MOON	**2** THURSDAY
31 TUESDAY	**3** FRIDAY
1 WEDNESDAY	**4** SATURDAY
	5 SUNDAY LAST QUARTER

Anthemis tinctoria 'Sauce Hollandaise' and *Crocosmia* 'Lucifer' in the orange border outside the Orangery

AUGUST

WEEK 32

6 MONDAY · Summer Bank Holiday, Scotland and Republic of Ireland

10 FRIDAY

7 TUESDAY

11 SATURDAY

8 WEDNESDAY

12 SUNDAY · NEW MOON

9 THURSDAY

The architectural plan of the basement of Chiswick House, in London, built by the 3rd Earl of Burlington in 1725, was the source for the design in box in the West Garden. The pond represents the dome.

AUGUST

WEEK 33

13 MONDAY

16 THURSDAY

14 TUESDAY

17 FRIDAY

15 WEDNESDAY

18 SATURDAY

19 SUNDAY

Annual clary (*Salvia viridis*)

AUGUST

20 MONDAY	**24** FRIDAY
21 TUESDAY	**25** SATURDAY
22 WEDNESDAY	**26** SUNDAY
23 THURSDAY	

FIRST QUARTER

The orange borders later in the season, with helenium, *Achillea filipendulina* 'Gold Plate' and the flowers of bronze fennel

AUGUST ∾ SEPTEMBER

27 MONDAY — Summer Bank Holiday, UK (exc. Scotland)

28 TUESDAY — FULL MOON

29 WEDNESDAY

30 THURSDAY

31 FRIDAY

1 SATURDAY

2 SUNDAY — Father's Day, Australia and New Zealand

Clockwise from top left: single *Dahlia* 'Moonfire'; Small Cactus *D.* 'Hayley Jane'; Medium Decorative *D.* 'Neal Gillson'; Small Semi-cactus *D.* 'Match'

SEPTEMBER

WEEK 36

3 MONDAY   Holiday, Canada (Labour Day) and USA (Labor Day) | **7** FRIDAY

4 TUESDAY   LAST QUARTER | **8** SATURDAY

5 WEDNESDAY | **9** SUNDAY

6 THURSDAY

Eighteenth-century lead urns on the South Front with *Verbascum bombyciferum*, which self-seeds among the flagstones

SEPTEMBER

WEEK 37

10 MONDAY

13 THURSDAY   Jewish New Year (Rosh Hashanah)

First Day of Ramadân (subject to sighting of the moon)

11 TUESDAY   NEW MOON

14 FRIDAY

12 WEDNESDAY

15 SATURDAY

16 SUNDAY

Cosmos bipinnatus 'Sea Shells' and *C. b.* 'Purity' with *Cleome hassleriana*
'Pink Queen' in the Kitchen Garden border

SEPTEMBER

WEEK 38

17 MONDAY

21 FRIDAY

18 TUESDAY

22 SATURDAY   Jewish Day of Atonement (Yom Kippur)

19 WEDNESDAY   FIRST QUARTER

23 SUNDAY   Autumnal Equinox

20 THURSDAY

The front garden of the Cottage Garden in September. 'Coltness Gem' dahlias, the delight of butterflies and bees, fill the box-edged beds.

SEPTEMBER

WEEK 39

24 MONDAY

27 THURSDAY — Jewish Festival of Tabernacles (Succoth), First Day

25 TUESDAY

28 FRIDAY

26 WEDNESDAY — FULL MOON

29 SATURDAY — Michaelmas Day

30 SUNDAY

Looking towards the stables in early evening sun with white *Cleome hassleriana* 'Helen Campbell' in the foreground

OCTOBER

WEEK 40

1 MONDAY

5 FRIDAY

2 TUESDAY

6 SATURDAY

3 WEDNESDAY   LAST QUARTER

7 SUNDAY

4 THURSDAY   Jewish Festival of Tabernacles (Succoth), Eighth Day

The view to Blanche's Vase along the Broad Walk and up the beech avenue. Blanche was the much-loved wife of the 6th Duke's heir. When she died aged twenty-eight she was mourned by her uncle with this magnificent memorial.

OCTOBER

---

8 MONDAY   Holiday, Canada (Thanksgiving Day)
                                                     Holiday, USA (Columbus Day)

11 THURSDAY   NEW MOON

9 TUESDAY

12 FRIDAY

10 WEDNESDAY

13 SATURDAY

14 SUNDAY

The Kitchen Garden at prime harvest time. There were three reasons why I yearned to grow vegetables. Greed was one. Another was for their own intrinsic beauty and the third was to make something out of nearly nothing.

OCTOBER

WEEK 42

15 MONDAY

19 FRIDAY   FIRST QUARTER

16 TUESDAY

20 SATURDAY

17 WEDNESDAY

21 SUNDAY

18 THURSDAY

'Muscat of Alexandria' grapes, a speciality at Chatsworth, lined up for final choice for the RHS Fruit Show

OCTOBER

WEEK 43

22 MONDAY Holiday, New Zealand (Labour Day)	**25** THURSDAY
23 TUESDAY	**26** FRIDAY FULL MOON
24 WEDNESDAY United Nations Day	**27** SATURDAY
	28 SUNDAY British Summertime ends

The Ring Pond, with water spouting from the beak of a seventeenth-century lead duck, and the Serpentine Hedge, planted in 1953

OCTOBER NOVEMBER

WEEK 44

29 MONDAY   Holiday, Republic of Ireland | **2** FRIDAY

30 TUESDAY | **3** SATURDAY

31 WEDNESDAY   Hallowe'en | **4** SUNDAY

1 THURSDAY   All Saints' Day
LAST QUARTER

Liquidambar styraciflua in the arboretum

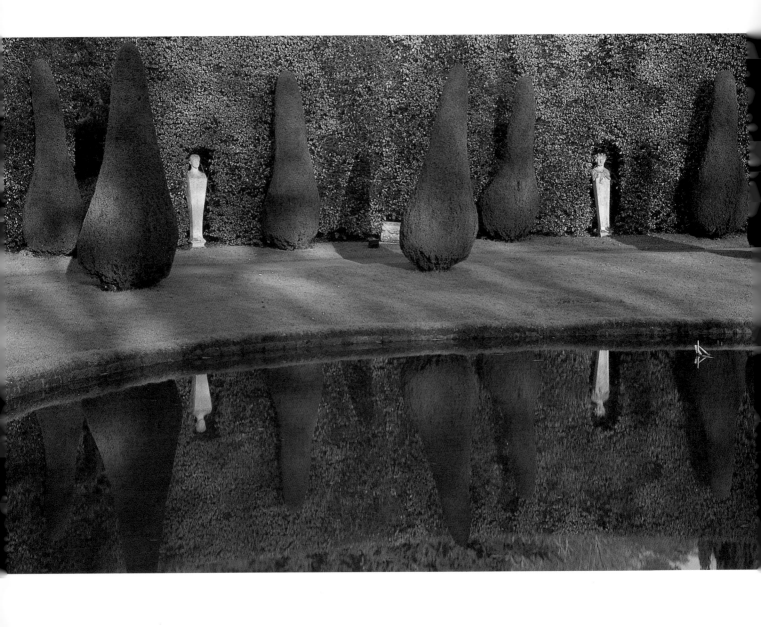

NOVEMBER

5 MONDAY   Guy Fawkes' Day

8 THURSDAY

6 TUESDAY

9 FRIDAY   NEW MOON

7 WEDNESDAY

10 SATURDAY

11 SUNDAY   Remembrance Sunday, UK
Holiday, Canada (Remembrance Day) and USA (Veterans' Day)

The Ring Pond, surrounded by clipped and bound Irish yews and a high beech hedge. The stone herms that stand against it were brought from Chiswick House.

NOVEMBER

12 MONDAY

16 FRIDAY

13 TUESDAY

17 SATURDAY   FIRST QUARTER

14 WEDNESDAY

18 SUNDAY

15 THURSDAY

The Spanish chestnut tree (*Castanea sativa*) planted in 1816 by
Grand Duke Nicholas of Russia, who became Czar in 1825

NOVEMBER

19 MONDAY	**22** THURSDAY Holiday, USA (Thanksgiving Day)
20 TUESDAY	**23** FRIDAY
21 WEDNESDAY	**24** SATURDAY FULL MOON
	25 SUNDAY

The Emperor Fountain in the Canal. It has reached a height of nearly 300 feet.

NOVEMBER DECEMBER

26 MONDAY

30 FRIDAY   St Andrew's Day

27 TUESDAY

1 SATURDAY   LAST QUARTER

28 WEDNESDAY

2 SUNDAY   Advent Sunday

29 THURSDAY

Looking from the Rock Garden down to the Ring Pond surrounded by a high beech hedge. Edensor church spire is just visible in the background.

DECEMBER

3 MONDAY

6 THURSDAY

4 TUESDAY

7 FRIDAY

5 WEDNESDAY   Jewish Festival of Chanukah, First Day

8 SATURDAY

9 SUNDAY   NEW MOON

The Strid in the Rock Garden, designed by Joseph Paxton in the 1840s. The Strid is named for the famous place on the River Wharfe at Bolton Abbey in Yorkshire.

DECEMBER

WEEK 50

10 MONDAY

11 TUESDAY

12 WEDNESDAY

13 THURSDAY

14 FRIDAY

15 SATURDAY

16 SUNDAY

Hamamelis × intermedia 'Pallida'. There is a large planting of this witch hazel on the east bank of the Grotto Pond.

DECEMBER

WEEK 51

17 MONDAY   FIRST QUARTER

20 THURSDAY

18 TUESDAY

21 FRIDAY

19 WEDNESDAY

22 SATURDAY   Winter Solstice

23 SUNDAY

The North Front of the house floodlit for Christmas visitors

DECEMBER

WEEK 52

24 MONDAY

Christmas Eve
FULL MOON

25 TUESDAY

Christmas Day
Holiday, UK, Republic of Ireland, Canada,
USA, Australia and New Zealand

26 WEDNESDAY

Boxing Day (St Stephen's Day)
Holiday, UK, Republic of Ireland, Canada,
Australia and New Zealand

27 THURSDAY

28 FRIDAY

29 SATURDAY

30 SUNDAY

A Christmas wreath of evergreen foliage and pine cones gathered
in the garden and decorated with baubles and ribbon, on a wall in
the stableyard

DECEMBER  JANUARY

WEEK 1

31 MONDAY   New Year's Eve
                                                LAST QUARTER

3 THURSDAY

1 TUESDAY   New Year's Day
        Holiday, UK, Republic of Ireland, Canada,
            USA, Australia and New Zealand

4 FRIDAY

2 WEDNESDAY   Holiday, Scotland and New Zealand

5 SATURDAY

6 SUNDAY   Epiphany

A seventeenth-century female figure holding a lyre marks the way
from the Kitchen Garden on to the Green Drive.

NOTES